A graduate of both the University of Iowa's Writers Workshop and the University of East Anglia, Gary Kissick has served as Editor of the *Hawaii Review* and has published poems, essays and stories in *Ambit, Antioch Review, Appalachian Review, Bamboo Ridge, Esquire, Literary Review, Manoa, The Nation, Poetry Now, Prairie Schooner, Rock Salt Plum, Rolling Stone, Spiked, The San Francisco Chronicle, White Noise* and numerous other journals and anthologies. Honours have included a National Endowment for the Arts Creative Writing Fellowship and a PEN Syndicated Fiction Award. His first book of poetry, *Outer Islands*, was published by the University of Hawaii Press after winning the first Pacific Poetry Competition. His comic novel *Winter in Volcano* was published by Hutchinson in 1999. He now resides in Norfolk, where he's writing a second novel, *Please Set Me Free So I Can Destroy The Earth*.

ANOTHER
KISSING
COUPLE
HAS
EXPLODED

Gary Kissick

Editor:
Ian Buck

**Editorial
Consultants:**
Tom Corbett   Helen Ivory

Gatehouse Team:
Jude Sayer   Charles Christian
Lee Seaman

GATEHOUSE PRESS LTD

Gatehouse Press Limited
Gatehouse @ Cargate Lane, Saxlingham Thorpe
Norfolk NR15 1TU

Gatehouse Press Online At:
www.gatehousepress.com

First Published in Great Britain by
Gatehouse Press Limited 2007

Printed and bound in Great Britain by
Biddles, King's Lynn

ISBN-10 (Paperback) 0 9554770 2 6
ISBN-13 (Paperback) 978 0 9554770 2 7
ISBN-10 (Hardback) 0 9554770 1 8
ISBN-13 (Hardback) 978 0 9554770 1 0

Cover design by Lee Seaman

With thanks to everyone involved in the production of this
book.

CONTENTS

i

Once we have children, nothing is ever the same. I lost my father in my infancy, and the birth of my son many years later somehow closed that broken circle and made me whole. He opened the vault of my heart, and for the first time in my life I learned what true love was. Nevertheless, at the time of his conception in Tirrenia, a stone's throw from Pisa, life seemed fraught with difficulty and uncertainty. My wife and I had packed all our belongings into a Ford Fiesta and driven from the ordered country of Germany to the culture shock of Italy, where we discovered that we had no place to live, that communication was difficult (even between us), that my teaching job was not the plum I had hoped it would be, and that a horde of Communists were about to descend on the town for a convention, making even hotel rooms impossible to find. It was only through bribery that we managed to secure a comfortable flat not far from the Tyrrenian Sea. And it was there and in Pisa that I tried to work out whether we were living in beauty or squalor, hope or despair. I've tried to capture the emotional contradictions that accompanied Dean's conception in the poem "101 Lines for My Son," which embodies what I hope to achieve in my longer poems: to passionately employ rhyme, rhythm, meter and other musical devices while eschewing fixed form, varying form and pace as the mood suits me, as in rhythmic jazz, without descending to the formlessness of free verse. I hope you find the poem worthy, son. Many of us know how our parents met, but few of us know the facts of our creation. It is, after all, an awkward subject.

While teaching at Upper Heyford, I took two of my most promising writing students to a gathering of poets that I had read convened monthly in a pub in Oxford. The pub, it turned out, was closed for repairs, but we were directed to some shabby liquorless hall where we found the poets who, despite their Oxford connections, seemed all a bit shabby themselves, dressing in worn and torn clothes as if to hide their privileged backgrounds. They seemed both delighted and surprised to see us, especially the women, for Dana and

Ray were handsome young men, and we were struck by their lack of reserve, especially that of one wild-haired girl, perhaps in her twenties, who bounded about in frabjous joy grasping our shoulders and exclaiming how wonderful it was that we had come. Dana seemed bemused, as was I, while the normally imperturbable Ray retreated behind folded arms. One young hussy sat on her boyfriend's lap and the two seemed to be working hard to make us envious or simply disgusted. A bearded man in a black turtleneck and jeans announced that it was time to begin, and a big-bellied man with a face as ugly as a sweet potato read a short poem that sounded like a soufflé of yearning. It was hard to find a word or image that one might get a grip on. The critical response seemed equally vague, though I gathered the poem was part of a series of such poems, one sigh in a vast miasma of sighs. The next poem, a much longer one, read by a pinched woman in thick glasses, moved as slowly as a revolving restaurant in fog. One reached the ends of lines having forgotten how they'd begun. Awkward and obscure poems followed. When it was my turn to read, I decided to wow the Oxfordians with an impassioned reading of "101 Lines for My Son." So I did. The girl who had grasped our shoulders was in rapture. She gasped in admiration and repeatedly interrupted the poem with cries of "You're so strong! You're so strong!" I assured her this was not the case. Had she missed the line about going mad? Nevertheless, I counted the poem a great success and left that night in triumph, having conquered the Oxford poetry circle, odd though it might have been. One week later Dana informed me he'd heard from a reliable source that that particular group of Oxford poets was best noted for living together under a bridge.

The lips that grace this cover are those of Jane Howarth, a friend of many years. They were chosen by the staff of Gatehouse Press from a numerous collection of lip imprints gathered at a party celebrating the earning of my PhD. I was impressed by the number of high-quality submissions, but remain disturbed by how many men donned lipstick in a desperate grab at immortality. They know who they are.

Gary Kissick, June 2007

Resignation
by Po Chui-i (772-846)

Don't think of things past and done;
dwelling on the past wakes regret.

Don't think of that yet to come;
the future will only dismay you.

Better, by day, to sit in your chair like a sack.
Better, by night, to lie in your bed like a stone.

When food comes, open your mouth.
When sleep comes, close your eyes.

Haleakala

Shall I throw myself
into the bottomless pit,
having braved this desert
to stand upon the brink?

Two hippies did once
— took the plunge —
their rightful children tightly
wrapped in their arms.

And long before them, the ancients
— bound in tapa, dutifully blessed —
were spirited swiftly
from curses.

Now all fall through darkness —
race of bones,
family of five . . . .

Into the abyss
I toss a stone
quickly quenched
by silence.

Tonight the stars will resume
their static journey,
presumably hurtling through space.

Some thoughts one can only
stand on the edge of.

To My Father

Not much to go on,
little to treasure.
A few photographs. A few tales.
The one where you save the water
at Guadalcanal is a wonder.
Or fooling the censor with Grandma —
you spelling 'Monday' with u, and she
scouring a map to find Munda.
Or the one where you fall off the wall,
drinking with Grandpa, the guzzler.

In the snaps you're courageously tall,
a dashing Marine or a father.
In one I'm a sack in your arms,
the beauty beside you is Mother,
the war's over, you're back on the farm,
and the clean slate you stand on is Iowa.

It's the very last likeness of you.

I'm 54 now.
You're 21.
But you're still the father,
and I'm still the son.

Last Christmas, I flew home, and talk
turned, like a page, to the past.
Searching a shoe box of Kodaks
for a picture of Mom in her class,
we found one of you in New Guinea,
devilishly handsome in khaki,
dwarfing the savage beside you.
At first it seemed two men, not three.
Mom had never seen clearly, and I
had never seen this one at all.

There stood the man she would marry,
the teenaged Marine, fit and grinning,
and there, grinning too, stood the savage,
bowlegged, stout, and tattooed,
with bones in his nose, and a necklace of bones,
a tufted grass skirt, and a flute.

But that was no flute.
And that was no coconut.
There were two grainy smiles
and one blot.

Your postwar bride failed to see
the truncated ghost at your feet.
Only me —
I alone saw all three dead.
Only for me rose the well-balanced truth
of you,
the headhunter,
the head.

Unpacking the Box

The house martins nesting high in the shed
shat on it all last summer
as if they were shags on a wave-battered stack
off Lindisfarne or Lunga.

They shat on the box called My Father,
a reliquary I've carried
from one Viking raid to another
as each last address burns behind me.

They'll not shit on My Father again,
for I intend to open,
discover and confront him.

Even the casket of Cuthbert
came to rest on a high hill in Durham,
and we all know what marvels ensued:

his corpse proved incorruptible
and one couldn't approach his gospel
without triggering a miracle.

All I need now is a knife.

Slaughter

Murder comes as surely
as darkness to the night.
I turn on the light
and they freeze.
Enemy assesses
mortal enemy.

Bare-handed, swift-palmed, I attack,
cracking the crisp black back
of the larger, squelching the smaller
to shapeless stains.

Now, from behind canisters,
dish rack, dishes, cups,
from under toaster and coffeepot,
I flush them from their hiding spots
and crush them as they run.

Nor will I leave the wounded
writhing among crumbs.
I'll thoroughly dispatch
each between finger and thumb.

Thus I attack my poverty.

But what of their silence
in the din of slaughter —
that unbroken code
none can crack?
It's their carapace,
their shield of honor,
so that we hear nothing
and believe nothing
but that this soulless nemesis
will persist,
rebounding from defeat
as surely as victory,
with new troops resembling the dead,
so that once again we encounter
the same vanquished foe,
the same unspoken
demand to surrender,
to surrender,
to begin at last the atonement
for all our virulent
trespasses.

Freddy

First there was a darkened drive,
a fitful wind, dry leaves,
the lid of a trash can
rolling on the edge of a clang.

Then there was Freddy,
menacing and swiftly
slashing the screams
of his victim,
whose blood sprayed gratuitous
crimson.

He wore a slouched hat,
burning scars, sharpened
knives for fingers.

He could enter the house
through a dream, drift
through a room
on a feather, cut
and gouge
and dissever
without leaving
a clue
at the scene.

That summer, Freddy
slashed all the rage.
By late October,
he was the razor in our apples,
and in dark suburbia,
gangs of children were wearing his face.

The Garbage Man

I pity the poor garbage men
collecting garbage in cold rain,
with their only revenge
to bang metal cans
and scatter lids
like best-laid plans.

I lie in bed with my lover,
attentive to curses and loud commands.

Someday, this all will change.
Children will be good
for fear of
The Garbage Man.

Momma will say,
"Go to bed now,
or The Garbage Man
gonna getcha!"

You Were Lying on the Railroad Tracks

You were lying on the railroad tracks,
apparently drugged or exhausted.

I was riding my faithful horse Spot,
wronged in love and disgusted.

What had been a tornado was now a train,
fixed on you, yet impersonal.

What had been a rumble was now a roar,
increasingly inexorable.

What had been a distance and a sporting chance
had now contracted to happenstance.

I spurred Spot to the spot and leap
heroically to your rescue,

sweeping you up and off the tracks
before the cowcatcher decked you.

Those are the facts, the rest is history —
marriage, two kids, a divorce —

and the worst has been, at least for me,
the eponymous fate of my horse.

Dali Prepares to Meet Gala on the Beach

All night I shimmered
with the maggots of fate,
restless as a carcass
distracted from quiescence.

The stone balloon of the moon made me anxious.

At the yolk of dawn I took my finest
hand-stitched chemise from Seville
and cut off a wide swathe until
it fell happily short of my navel.

I tore a silken hole for my shoulder,
a single tear exposing one nipple,
and a final curt rent in the middle
revealing the hairs of my chest.

I was greatly perplexed by the collar—
to leave it open, like a flower, or intact?
I circumcised it with scissors, then closely
shaved the damp shameful pits of my arms.

But this fell short of the ideal blue
I'd seen in Seville's senoritas,
the hard-shelled blue of a clam,
eternity fused with cyan,

so I mixed laundry bluing with powder
and dyed my pits with this.
I soon boiled over like chowder
as a river of blue ran through

the milky white silk of my shirt.
I shaved once more with conviction
till the peat of my pits ran with blood.
This I daubed on my cheeks for complexion.

Then wishing for carnal cologne,
I sought the ordure of a ram
when the dank night steams
and dung hums.

This pleased but remained incomplete.
I brewed a pot of donkey glue
and stirred in fists of mered,
which proved quite delightful when cooled.

Thus anointed, I awaited
our preordained appointment
like a watch awaits the heat.

Then it was she on the beach —

a glint of the moon facing waves
like a widow, her legs
two spoons, her back
a window.

And the curve of her spine and her shoulders,
and the exposed blue nape of her neck,
left me ravished, deranged, and ashamed
of my Cadaverous fecklessness.

Smelling like a goat, I undressed,
washed away my pungent bouquet,
donned my dead mother's necklace,
and pinned in my hair a narcissus.

And there she stood, the edge of a cliff,
and I a precipitous cyclist
careering toward the blissful abyss,
a narcissist hurtling towards Isis.

It was then that I realized the need
for handlebars to grip in such crisis.

for Sharon

I know I said I loved
Helena Bonham Carter,
but since I've met you, Sharon,
I've gone off her.

It's true I said I hated
that shameless whore Madonna,
but since you said you like her,
I've gone on her.

Your pin-up boy
is love's hegemonic:
Darcy dripping
pride and prejudice.

The wounded voice
of Bobby Dylan
you called a cow
in need of killing.

Twice forever.
Two divorces.
One's much safer betting
on horses.

Love's a menace.
Love's a yoke.
Love's an egg
in tennis.

Let's break it gently
to our frail mothers first.
Then I'll call Helena,
you Colin Firth.

After Lu Che

The silk of her sleeve
in a fallen leaf.
Dust on the stones.
Bars on the door.
Loving once
and never more.

Koran

If a man marries the woman he loves,
into whom does he make his pillow?

Another Kissing Couple Has Exploded

There's a face on Neptune
just like the one
on the moon, and Mars, and Venus,
and another kissing couple
has exploded.

Witnesses claim
they embraced in spring rain
— he raised her chin,
she spoke his name —
their lips touched,
they felt too much —
the bliss of one kiss,
then a tongue of pure flame.

There's a face in the mirror
much like the one
on Neptune, and Venus, and Mars.
And time, they say, will heal all wounds.
But wounds can leave such scars.

These cratered eyes
will never change;
they cast
eternal shadows.
These lips will never
turn to flames.
Such space
cannot be traveled.

But a rich, supple emollient,
a light, creamy emulsion,
a collagen-based miracle gel
applied to the face in the mirror
might erase every trace of a tear or
turn shadow to light — who can tell?

Who can tell what stain on the wall
will glow with the eyes of Jesus?
Who can tell what UFO
contains the soul of Elvis?
The Virgin Mary has cured with tears
believers paralyzed for years.

Distress signals
from a dying planet
reach our own
and go unanswered,
and one in every two of us
is not a true human being at all,
but something like an incubus
that drinks what love is left in us.

One reads of others' misery.
One tragic girl eats cutlery.
She swallows whole the fork and knife,
and eats the meaning of her life.

A child is murdered by children,
snatched and dispatched in an hour,
or a baby is found in the morning dew,
fixed to the corpse of his mother.

Christ, it makes me want to scream,
like fetal cells in beauty cream —
his lips touched hers,
they were warm, they were lovers,
and that was all, and all they recovered
was less than the sum of two shadows.

God what I'd give
to so combust,
ignite with a kiss
and burn with lust,
and when they sift
through rain-washed dust,
not an eyelash of us
will remain.

Dust to dust,
ashes to ashes.
Understanding is what
the world surpasses.

And now they say another planet
circles beyond all other planets,
and was always there,
a blot in the dark,
a masked voyeur at the window.

This could explain the mysteries
that plague our species like disease —
the scores abducted every day,
freeze-dried babies sold as slaves,
the missing brain of JFK,
and the inner voice speaking our name.

The moon's a very quiet place
where nothing is eroded.
Forever wears a tragic face
mirrored by an empty space.
And another kissing couple
has exploded.

101 Lines for My Son (conceived near Pisa)

When your mother first aroused me
in the kitchen of the casa
on Via Del Acacie,
it was fall, rent was cheap,
walls were mildewed, shutters green.
All in all, it was lovely . . .

though impetuous guns cracked the dawn,
ridding the sky of songbirds,
and deprived of both wingspread and song,
that ardent sky broke into storm.
When lightning slashed the shutter slats,
our nights collapsed like shattered glass.

As I've said, I was content,
though evenings soon depressed me.
At times I thought I'd go quite mad.
The food was good, the water bad.
Dull drums of guns bloodied dawn.
The slightest death upset me.

I was writing songs of life,
songs of myself, songs in which
winter flung the ravished sea
upon the shore and left her.
Hunger drove me to the kitchen.
There I met your mother.

Shutters swung open, the sun shone warm —
call it reckless abandon.
Galileo's come and gone,
yet falling bodies carry on.
Upon a spinning earth, beneath a chandelier,
one bit the other's ear.

Yes, the tower truly rose
over Duomo and Baptistry
the day your mother first aroused
your father from his sophistry.
The solipsism I espoused
was only rigid fallacy.

And I confess sometimes I'd freely
identify with that campanile —
vertiginous with sheer desire,
immortal for another hour,
rising like a sacred spire,
leaning toward a pizza parlor.

Capricious air hummed cappuccino,
the breeze the sweetest dolce,
the day desire spoke bambino
in mortal sotto voce.
We gathered shells beneath the sea,
where every wind's a mystery.

The shutters flew like violent books,
a hot breath of libretto.
We sang that song until it broke,
adagio to presto,
that day your mother first awoke
the dormant song in petto.

You were composed one month before
damage inflicted on the door
of the kitchen in the casa
blanca on Via Del Acacie.
Those days I hurled glasses more.
Love's a virgin, sex a whore.

Quaint, somehow, the time we took
to revel in some torn piazza,
to seek out every ochre nook,
caress each egg of alabaster.
Two nightingales hung on a hook,
a miniature disaster.

And I still see a bloodied rabbit
hung in plastic among the un-
plucked trussed ducks and chickens,
larks, quails and woodcocks,
partridges and pigeons.
It was the changing of the seasons.

We lived in the Quattro Stagioni
upon the Piazza Miracoli,
in the reflections of the Arno,
Marina di Pisa,
San Piero a Grado,
beside the Tyrannical Sea.

The alleys stank, the air was quick,
the cost of living lyrical.
When announced, you seemed at first
an error purely clerical.
As I've said, I was content
to pay my songs, compose the rent.

Thus should you bear one sullen gene,
one thorn from the crown of Jesus,
forgive me, Son, it came from me;
it pricks us as it pleases.
You'll find the quay severe and worn
where Byron penned the famed Don Juan.

Headless saints unbowed by fear
might find a way to make this clear,
but with my head held in my hands,
I find myself a headless man.

We composed our operetta
while rain fell through a green umbrella
upon a street with no acacia.

The shutters swung open, the rains were warm,
our pleasures irretrievable,
as we clung one to one that dawn
to conceive the inconceivable.

The Emperor of Wine

There's much to be said for much wine.
The banished immortal Li Po
drank it to the bottom of truth
and now knows what Kiang River knows.

He knew the heart of the river merchant's wife
and the solace of wind in tall pines.
He knew rivers never returned from the sea,
but he best knew the wisdom of wine.

Poems in pocket, dagger in sleeve,
he thought life a dream one drank up.
He found clear visions high in the mountains,
high visions deep in his cup.

One cup, and one sings a song.
Two cups, and one writes a poem.
Three cups, one's one with the Tao.
Four cups approach the unknown.

He once said in jest that he wished
to be faithfully forever attended
by a maid with wine, and a maid with a spade
to bury him wherever he ended.

An invitation to the Imperial Palace
found Li Po meditating supine.
"Please excuse me, my Lord," he responded.
"Your humble servant's an emperor of wine."

Li Po sketched a scene in a stroke,
and the world in no more than twelve lines.
He set all his poems afloat
on a clear stream that flowed from the vine.

One night, on the river, entranced,
Li Po the philosopher found
that truth can be deep when he stooped
to scoop the moon from the water and drowned.

Our Rural Idyll

The night you eyed the tea towel
lining the breadbasket, I thought
you were working out its art,
it being a new and somewhat flash
abstract of a halibut, from Habitat.

'Did you know that halibut
means holy flatfish?' I asked.

'Holy flatfish my ass,' you said coldly.
'Look. Look closely.'

I'd opened it in half
like a crisply creased map,
it being a stiff, unyielding linen,
yet along one crease it was tattered.
It looked, in fact, half-eaten,
much like the bread in your hand.

'You took that towel from the larder
the mice tried to nest in.
I've been eating rodent-
infested ciabatta.'

'Yes,' I confessed, 'but—'

'And there's poison in there as well!'

That night you took ill, doubled up
like a deck chair in a gale,
and if looks could kill,
Morse and The Bill
would be digging the garden right now.

The towel, when unfolded,
was Rorschach origami,
a flatfish in a crossfire
between the mob and a tsunami.

The way I see it,
our plague-free life thereafter
has been a loan fate's forgotten.

And, you must admit,
among the pipes and ill-fit cupboards,
there is not a crack you could squeeze a mouse through
that has not been sealed with sealant
or bunged with boards and glue,
and has been since that night I found you
screaming barefoot in the dark in the kitchen.

Confession

Even with night lights the long haul
from bedroom to loo between cold walls
is a monk's procession
through the Devil's darkness.

We want no more surprises,
no fur and teeth beneath our feet,
nothing scurrying, squealing, or worse.

That's why I've concealed,
from you who insist on truth,
what I now, reluctantly, reveal —

that after sealing the house like a mummy's tomb,
plugging each gap with toxic foam,
stopping with bricks the secret passage
that runs like a shortcut in Clue,
baiting the cupboards, setting the traps
— after making it thoroughly mouse-proof —

I awoke the next day to a mouse,
sniffing by the bed,
which I hit on the head with a shoe
repeatedly till dead.

Then I buried the corpse in the garden,
scrubbed the blood from the rug,
rolled my secret in a ball
and swallowed it whole until now.

Such shocks, I admit, constrict one's reach,
affect the way one throws a switch
or addresses the floor with one's feet.

You claim the truth is always best.
I say it's often better.
But never wake a sleepwalker
walking upon water.

Consider Calvin struggling
to open the one eye sealed shut
and discovering what live weight had sealed it.

Consider Claire awakening
to find what she found in her hair.

We've fared much better,
and if you've failed to hear
of rats that drag the ducklings under
and savage the runts at lambing
— or the ghost in the wallboard
above our headboard
gnawing each night before dawn —
then that's better, too, than the truth.

Degrees

'No heat!' Thus am I roused
from my sleep, warm bed,
and complacency — the radiators colder
than a dead man's cheek,
each one a slab in the morgue.

No sound, no reassuring
hum of the boiler,
an icebreaker shaking awake
to cleave the reticent dawn.
Yet the light's on. The electrics work.
It's as if we have

'No oil!' We've been reading it wrong
all winter. The landlord said
it would last through spring,
yet we've barely passed
December,
and the ice is thickening.

Beneath each foundation
lies a fact of nature,
a simple permafrost of truth:
Cold in winter.

And colder still, with worse to come,
if warming sheets of Arctic ice
tumble in the gears of the Gulf Stream
and quietly subvert it.

'You needn't be so glum,' you chide.
'You're always so extreme. Besides,
deprived of global warming,
we have the wood stove to keep us alive.'

No wood. Bits of kindling, yes,
but no combustibles from verdant forests
that carpet the hills of Norfolk
right up to the tree line. Thus,

no fire. You take refuge
in the electric shower. I turn on the stove.
And if push comes to shove I suppose I could wash
dirty clothes and run the dryer.

You boil breakfast,
hold an egg to each cheek,
don Shetland wool,
fog the mirror.

Somehow you manage.
Better the car once defrosted.
Better the classrooms on campus.

I crawl back to bed with the phone
and like a polar bear go with the floe,
adrift in my insular den.

By nine I've struck oil.
But not today. Come Monday.
Then there'll be air to bleed,
and, of course, my wallet.

I call for wood.
The woodsman's heard
of neither cord nor pallet.

'We sell it by the Toyota,' he says.
'I've not heard these newfangled terms.'

I order one Toyota,
or in Old Church Slavonic,
a shitload. We'll see it Monday,
when the world resumes.

At night, limb by limb,
we feed the Christmas tree to the fire,
like a god who has died for our sins.

The brittle needles sparkle
and the blue spruce cracks,
eagerly flashing to ashes.

We ransack the house
for anything flammable.
Danielle Steele burns well
as I'm sure she will in Hell.

We need to get back to normal —
me asleep in flannel sheets,
having already earned my degrees,
and you up at five, with coffee and heat,
poring sweat over Dante's Inferno.

In a Pisan Albergo

I. Menu

Dear foreigner and guest in the sunny Italy:
the spaghetti are not to be cut for making them
shorter.
Not with the fork,
so much less so the knife.
You ought not to help yourself
with the spoon for rolling them up.
It is sufficient to seize
with the slender point of the fork,
supported by the plate's concavity.
They will form a bite just right
for your legendary mouth.

II. Hallway Notice

Fire! It is what can doing
we hope. No fear! Not ourselves.
Say quietly to all people
coming up down everywhere a prayer.
Always is a clerk, a man
assured of safety by expert men
who are in the bar
to telephone for fighters
of the fire to come out!

Exquisitely Close to Almost
or
Je Ne L'ai Plus Jamais

I was cycling
through southern France
with two pairs of pants,
all alone.

She was doing
song and dance
in the papal palace
of Avignon.

It was Figaro
and Don Giovanni,
La Mort de Didon and
Les Hommes Sont Bêtes.

Some note shook
my Aqua Libre
and caused my bottle
to effervesce.

And strung between
both ears a string
resonated
with sweet vibration.

We met that night
in a warm café
over candlelight
and expectation.

On ne sait jamais.
On ne sait jamais.
She chose the tune
and I drank it.

I had the Poulet
Sauté
Enchanté,
and she had the Poussins
Grillé
aux Poireaux
with Rouget
Grillé
au Poivre Vert.

After the Tulipes
à la Glace
Pralinée,
after café,
Grand Marnier
and the bill,

a little bird
she couldn't kill
peeped out a small
"Ecoutez . . . ."

"Je ne pourrais
jamais
parler
Anglais,"
she tensed.

And I,
dismayed,
having al-
ready paid,
could certainly
never
speak French.

Pick Your Own

People ask how long they'll last,
and I say, 'Do I look like a prophet?'

But now I know.
Some have spots
you could slip a finger in,
and others have burns
rough as warts.

Two more weeks
they'll be done.
Too much rain,
too much sun.

That's the way it is with strawbs.
Some years they roll on and on
like the endless queues at Wimbledon,
and the cows make double cream.
And other years the ground's
as tough and stingy
as a puckered bean,
and just walking on it
gives you haricot veins.

This is hard country for strawbs.
Look around. All corn.

The nub of the problem is this —
they count the raindrops.
One too many,
they go pwidgy.
One too few,
they go radishy —
round and red
but hard-hearted.

Please, don't get me started.
Even in a good year
you can't sell a turnip to Tesco's
or the curmudgeons at Budgen's in Swaffham.

I offer them punnets
fit for the Queen Mother's palate,
and some numb-chance in a saw-pit
who doesn't know soft fruit from squit
says he can't buy from a local supplier,
his hands are tied from on high.

They buy a genetically modified strain
from a secret site in Spain
where they've replaced God's dirt and rain
with something like slurried pig's brains —
I'll tell you true I don't what he was on about,
but I says 'If it's shit for brains you want,
I see plenty of that here in Norfolk,'
and I give him a squint
like a worm on his fork.

Yisty, a gentleman asked
for fifty punnets for Sunday.
Said he'd send his kids 'round to pick 'em.

'Thanks, but no,' I said.
'That's an offer I'll refuse.'
Kids'll pick anything red.
They'll trod on a dozen
ripening virgins
to reach a sodden fat corpse
oozing rouge.

Well, he started putting on parts and —
Yes, yes, darling, of course you can.
I'm sorry. Didn't know you were in such a hurry.
Pound a punnet.
Everyone's busy these days.

At The Frog Crossing

Patience, I tell myself
at the frog crossing.
*Turn off the engine
and wait. Impediments
have impeded your progress before,
and though there's no end in sight
to your fate, these are more
or less in motion, lurch-
ing now and then like hearts
startled awake by emotion.*

But freight trains carting off regrets
lumber more speedily than these
ungainly green legions.
And though I'll get
where I must go — eventually —
this progress seems painfully slow.

Of course, one man's frog
is another's toad,
and I'm the clod
who chose this road.
A mile back I could have gone
direct instead of scenic.
But no, not me, I had to choose
the route that proves symbolic,
the proverbial road less travelled by.
Now I know why.

It may seem that frogs
migrating en masse
are dimwitted pinball,
leathery gas,
molasses reaching a critical mass,
or pea soup approaching a boil.

But sadly it's tragically deeper than that.
Here cross good intentions, fond wishes,
disloyal dreams and desires —
erratic, fickle, quixotic, obscene
tricksters, thieves, and liars.

Let them pass, in fits and starts —
cruel resolutions, sputtering farts,
each song unpenned for lack of tune,
each tale for lack of plot,
each drink drunk with hope before noon
in search of fierce inspiration,
and the sad little twitch of each little life
postponed till the next incarnation.

These are not scarlet
tree frogs whose toxins
tip the blow-darts and arrows
of exotic misfortune.

Nor are they frogs
whose secret secretions
one licks for mystic
hallucinations.

These are the mud-drab creatures of youth,
the prosaic, uncouth, common frogs,
whose young we scooped from native pools
when we, ourselves, were polliwogs.

They seemed like treasure then.
And we, so rich, released them.

Now here hop horny adolescent lusts
that I failed to outgrow when I grew.
And my maybe tomorrows and someday I musts
have thrown in their lot with this crew.

Here each bloated indecision
springs to fatuous conclusion.
Here certainty leapfrogs
under illusion.

There hops my first marriage
over my last.
The decision to chuck it.
The one to hold fast.

That fat one's my fondest ambition.
That desiccant black one's my soul
that I thought I might save from perdition,
till it shrank from my touch and grew cold.

There's a vow sealed with a kiss
that awaits the return of a princess.
And there, on the verge, growing old,
loiters that prodigal son, early promise.

Here hunker frogs that have squatted so long
on my life it's all pad and no pond.

And so it goes at the frog crossing,
one life delayed on a country road;
a scenic green Rorschach simply unfolds
to reveal one side much like the other.

And one acknowledges with wry smile
that this could take awhile.

Just Dawn

I lie awake and study you,
the face that floats upon your sleep
like a blanket of moonlight on snow.

In the wash of your eyes,
the stroke of your nose,
the down upon one burnished cheek,
I seek to decipher your soul.

This is your face without faces —
your circumflexed brow,
your scrunch of delight,
your smile endorsing what pleases.

This is the silent you,
the tidal you, the subtle
rise and fall of you,
the curtain drawn over the dream.

I gaze in admiration.

You open your eyes
and scream.

The Last Time

The last time I lived alone
was more than twenty years ago
in a termite-riddled house
on stilts in Honolulu.

The stairs were decayed.
The walls gave way
to a touch
like a faithless marriage.

I was never lonely.
I was never afraid.

Here the walls are strong
enough to resist my fists.
And the danger of the stairs is
that no one will ever climb them.

Elegy

Because she has died,
a branch breaks the moon.

ACKNOWLEDGMENTS

Acknowledgments are due to the editors of the following publications, in which some of these poems first appeared:

Rock Salt Plum (In A Pisan Albergo)

White Noise (The Emperor of Wine)

Constellation (Another Kissing Couple Has Exploded, Exquisitely Close to Almost or Je Ne L'ai Plus Jamais)

Bird Watching at Pagham Harbour

In the real world in which swallows
have forsaken Sussex for Africa
and house sparrows continue
their mysterious decline,
a hopeful blue dawn follows
the religiously cold rains of Christmas.

We walk briskly in wellies to mudflats—
a broken seawall, then a broad expanse
dotted with plovers and redshanks.

Cormorants yawn like cold flames.

A single cry neatly trebles the sky.

Soon we reach the sea,
whose merest glance is deep,
then drift apart like leaves,
each to a world pooled in wind:
the boy to collect whorled shells
cast on a shingle of flint,
the wife and I to that silence
that roars, like the ocean, within.

It's simple, bird watching.
At first one collects birds like coins,
counting, sorting, hoarding.

Then one collects birds like promises.

Then comes a dawn when one sees
that without birds life's a mirror
that wonders what it looks like;
that a gull's an arrangement
of wings, waves, and wind;
that turnstones all turn with the tide,
each aligned, no estrangement;
that while a dunlin is this,
and a sandpiper that,
no bird in the world is a word.

And one wonders how close
we might edge toward redemption
if we all nameless faced
one direction.

Elegy Wasted on Harry

Two feet under. Damn deep
for a hamster. Enough to keep
the ghost of Harry
flat as a sheet forever.

In human terms it's interment
in a mine shaft sealed with lead.

In practical terms, one could still
fork the bed for a fuchsia
without forking up Harry instead.

The horror that is Harry in decay
should stay mercifully far away
in the shade of the cross with his name.

He who used to climb our socks
was laid to rest in a cardboard box,
curled up so tight
his one white stripe
ran around him like a vicar's collar.

We wished him back,
our Houdini —
confined when we looked up,
at bay when we looked down.

He could mesmerize with tireless
tours of the maze of his cage,
then climb your inside trouser leg
while the treadmill wheel's still spinning.

Many's the time he'd insouciantly
brave the searchlight of the TV,
having tunneled out of Colditz
and climbed the Alps of the stairs.

And once as the boy lay sleeping
in a bed still wet with tears,
he awoke to a small mouth whispering
tender niblets in his ear.

"Harry!" he cried in delight.
"Mom! Dad! It's Harry!"

That was late last night.
We buried him last Friday.

Just Dawn

I lie awake and study you,
the face that floats upon your sleep
like a blanket of moonlight on snow.

In the wash of your eyes,
the stroke of your nose,
the down upon one burnished cheek,
I seek to decipher your soul.

This is your face without faces —
your circumflexed brow,
your scrunch of delight,
your smile endorsing what pleases.

This is the silent you,
the tidal you, the subtle
rise and fall of you,
the curtain drawn over the dream.

I gaze in admiration.

You open your eyes
and scream.

The Last Time

The last time I lived alone
was more than twenty years ago
in a termite-riddled house
on stilts in Honolulu.

The stairs were decayed.
The walls gave way
to a touch
like a faithless marriage.

I was never lonely.
I was never afraid.

Here the walls are strong
enough to resist my fists.
And the danger of the stairs is
that no one will ever climb them.

Elegy

Because she has died,
a branch breaks the moon.

ACKNOWLEDGMENTS

Acknowledgments are due to the editors of the following publications, in which some of these poems first appeared:

Rock Salt Plum (In A Pisan Albergo)

White Noise (The Emperor of Wine)

Constellation (Another Kissing Couple Has Exploded, Exquisitely Close to Almost or Je Ne L'ai Plus Jamais)